Sieon C. R

WHERE IS MY FATHER
The Missing Pattern

WHERE IS MY FATHER
The Missing Pattern

WHERE IS MY FATHER
The Missing Pattern

Published by Literacy in Motion
Phoenix, Arizona
www.AnthonyThigpen.com   .

Anthony KaDarrell Thigpen
Editor-in-Chief

Library of Congress Cataloging-in-Publication Data Publisher and Printing by Literacy in Motion
Cover Design by Literacy in Motion Design Team

WHERE IS MY FATHER
The Missing Pattern
ISBN: 978-1-7336583-1-7

Christian/Self-Help
Printed in the United States of America

WHERE IS MY FATHER
Sieon C. Roberts, Sr.

The Missing Pattern
Acknowledgements & Dedication

I would like to acknowledge my loving and faithful wife, Lady Anita Roberts and my children Giara, Leon, Sieon Jr. and Jeremiah, as well as my granddaughter Amyra. To my mom, Delpha Roberts. my sisters, Hawah, and Arkeya, thank you all for loving me unconditionally.

Again, thank you to my publisher and friend, who is more like a brother, Anthony KaDarrell Thigpen of Literacy in Motion. You are the one that has pushed, coached, and helped produced every publication and pieces of literature about my life. You are responsible for all the many newspaper articles, 4 books and countless professional photographs. I'm so thankful for your friendship and your unfailing acts of kindness toward me.

I am forever grateful to Pastor Keion Henderson, my cousin and brother in the gospel. You have been a powerful influence in my life. I sincerely value your input in this book. I cannot express how joyous my heart feels to be connected with family in ministry. We share an indescribable connection as there are so many parallels in our lives.

Lastly, I dedicate this book to the one who disciples me, my father in the gospel, Archbishop William Hudson, III. Thank you for your love, correction teaching and impartations. You have been a true, pure and consistent leader in my life.

Table of Content

Foreword p. 8 - 13
ROADMAP TO REWARDS
For Youth and Adults Seeking a Blueprint

Chapter 1/ p. 14 - 19
THE PATTERN
The DNA That Defines Our Destiny

Chapter 2/ p. 20 - 24
GENERATIONAL TRAITS
Breaking Unwanted Cycles

Chapter 3/ p. 25 - 31
THE POWER OF MY PAIN
Father of Many Nations

Chapter 4/ p. 32 - 35
DEADBEAT DADS
The Pattern, the Beat and the Rhythm

Chapter 5/ p. 36 - 42
CHILD SUPPORT VS. LIFE SUPPORT
The Consequences of Absent Fathers

Chapter 6/ p. 43 - 48
THE FATHER'S BLESSING
The Transfer from Fathers to Sons

Chapter 7/ p. 49 - 53
GOD IS MY FATHER
The Pattern of Prayer

Chapter 8/ p. 54 - 60
I AM ESTABLISHED
Amongst Two or Three Witnesses

Foreword

ROADMAP TO REWARDS

For Youth and Adults Seeking a Blueprint

FOREWORD

By William Hudson, III and Keion Henderson

William Hudson, III

One of the Greek words for father is *pater,* which means one who nourishes, protects and upholds. A father is the giver of seed, therefore a source of life. A father gives foundation and purpose. A father gives direction and structure. A father is a teacher, trainer and an example. When children have healthy relationships with their father they tend to be more confident, resourceful, economically savvy and productive.

My most impactful influence of fatherhood is being a father to all my spiritual sons. I have mentored many senior pastors and leaders by helping them find their purpose and passion. I am most fulfilled when I able to restore hope and give direction to those who have lost their way. Being a father blesses me as such as it blesses my spiritual sons – it gives me great joy. My assignment is to care, cover and correct sons and daughters until they are ready to be promoted into their assignment and destiny. My anointing is to prepare leaders and pass mantles to spiritual sons and daughters. I am only able to be a productive father in ministry because I had a strong spiritual father in my life as a pattern for fatherhood. Your pattern will determine your destiny.

Patterns are often provided by non-biological and spiritual fathers, as well as genetically. Blood type is determined by the father's bloodline, because dads provide the seed at conception. Therefore, we understand the role of a father as one providing identity to offspring. He also provides a sense of validation and assurance through affirmation and approval. Sometimes, God ordains spiritual fathers, mentors and guardians for such support.

The information in this book reveals just how significant a father's role is. This book, *Where is My Father,* is a tool for dads to perfect their fatherhood skills. Bishop Roberts is administering deep emotional healing to father's, sons and daughters.

I believe this book will break cycles of pain and create healthy patterns in families. This book will be used to strengthen marriages, families and relationships. This book reveals some of the root causes of why people suffer with rejection, depression and emptiness. Bishop Roberts provides solutions for tough issues and inspiration for fathers. He has a proficient writing style that any reader would enjoy.

Bishop Roberts sets a great example for fathers to follow. He has succeeded in life in spite of challenges with his own father and stepfather. He is a great husband, natural father, spiritual father and a father to many in his community. As your spiritual father in the ministry, I am so proud of you. Your labor of love, having written this book, will impact future fathers for decades to come.

Archbishop William Hudson, III serves as the presiding bishop of Pilgrim Assemblies International and is founder and overseer of Powerhouse Church in Chicago. His wife, Elder Andria Hudson currently serves as pastor of Powerhouse Church.

* * *

Keion Henderson

Rabbi Daniel Lapin, author of "Thou Shalt Prosper," says that Jews feel at ease blessing their children each Sabbath with the words: "May God make you like Ephraim and like Manasseh." He went on to say that Ephraim represents spiritual steadfastness and Manasseh represents economic creativity. With that in the backdrop, one of the highlights of my life took place in an expensively decorated conference room at The Hermitage Hotel in Nashville, Tennessee. I had an opportunity to ask Rabbi Lapin face to face, to not just explain the meaning of the aforementioned sentence, but to explain from a Jewish perspective the overall experience. He said, "Jewish fathers traditionally make it a habit of speaking this particular blessing over their children."

He then went on to say something I don't think I'll ever forget. He said, "If you want to disrupt a race, a community, or a home, you need only remove the father." History backs up this claim, whether considering slavery or the holocaust it has validity. With the stroke of a pen, Roberts has re-ignited the discussion of an ancient problem with a modern approach. The great Roman leader Julius Caesar recorded the earliest known version of the proverb, 'Experience is the teacher of all things,' in 'De Bello Civili' (c. 52 B.C.).

Roberts understands more than anyone, the debilitating effect that fatherlessness has on a child. In a sense, I believe it is what makes him such a great father and author today. It is my opinion that *Where is My Father*, is the roadmap to the reward that millions of youth and adults have been seeking. This book isn't about spitting vitriol, in fact, it's quite the opposite. Sieon Roberts shows us that there is an answer to the question, "Where is my father?" This book unfolds the reality that you can actually create an abundant life even if you've started with a parental deficit.

Pastor Keion Henderson, with the support of his wife, Felicia, is the senior pastor of the Lighthouse Church in the greater Houston area (Humble, Texas). For nearly a decade, he has faithfully served in ministry.

Chapter 1

THE PATTERN

The DNA That Defines Our Destiny

There are so many kind and loving people, that are not parents, giving guidance to children everyday. In our advanced society we have guardians, coaches, teachers, counselors, pastors, mentors and so many other professional and personal voices providing instruction. While these roles are critical for personal development, children need fathers. So, is there a different impact fathers impart above and beyond instructors? According to I Corinthians 4:15, there is a distinction between the idea of having instructors as opposed to fathers. *"For though ye have ten thousand instructors in Christ, yet have ye not many fathers: for in Christ Jesus I have begotten you through the gospel"* (I Corinthians 4:15). So what's the difference?

An instructor is one who teaches in various capacities. On the other hand, a father is someone who shows forth a pattern. Fatherhood defines a unique DNA that reveals the pattern to our destiny. Throughout this book, we will use the words *pattern* and *father* interchangeably. The DNA of a father produces a spiritually organic pattern that is duplicated in the life of his child. In many cases, this pattern is clearly seen even in the absence of one's biological father.

A pattern is a repeated decorative design or a model used as a guide. A father possesses the blueprint of his child's destiny –

whether present or absent this reality remains unaltered. One of the largest cries in our country is individuals that are desperate to discover their pattern. The lack of knowledge surrounding biological fathers has prompted a lost sense of identity, an emptiness, and a void for many.

Tests, Trials and Failures Are Inescapable, During Life's Journey.

Tests, trials and failures are inescapable, during life's journey. However, much pain could be avoided if fatherless individuals had a pattern to glean from. Unfortunately, Satan's scheme is to infuse his poisonous agenda to destroy the concept of functional God-ordained families. Even when believers follow God's perfect plan, that doesn't produce perfect people, it merely etches a pattern into every home.

There are so many mainstream influences and statistical stimuli that perpetuate single-parent homes. As a result, many fathers easily deviate from Gods original intent for family. In other words, fatherlessness has become the norm in our society. More than 20 million children live without the presence of their biological fathers. About 57% of African-Americans, 31% of Hispanics, and 20% of Caucasians are foreign to their fathers.

More Than 20 Million Children Live Without the Presence of Their Biological Fathers.

When such behavior becomes the norm, it also suits what is socially acceptable. As a result, so many children have no pattern, and others mimic a pattern that is not their own. This grueling concept leaves children confused and wandering.

A lost sense of identity does immeasurable internal damage before an individual even realizes it. Afterward, disappointment, anger and hurt causes most fatherless children to deny the need of their dads. If a father's role was merely designed to insure success, many could argue that they successfully thrived and beat the odds. Our argument is not centered on success alone, rather the original blueprints of human identity.

A simple hair follicle can reveal relevant information about our genetic DNA. Likewise, the presence of a father exudes an essence that gives children added purpose. Even when fathers are absence, children unintentionally and unknowingly immolate patterns of their behavior – this is often called genetics or non-sensory behavior. When God created man, he made us in his image and after his likeness. According to Genesis 1:26-27, God breathed the breath of life in mankind, and then we became living souls. In other words, even though relationship allows listeners to learn God's statutes and ways, non-believers will exhibit characteristics of God. This is because God made us like himself.

I spent all of my childhood and most of my life without a pattern. The substitute pattern provided was a poor alternative. The men that had the opportunities to father me ended up hurting or leaving me. Such is the case with so many fatherless individuals. This resulted in extreme hurt, anger and mistakes. I even made two suicide attempts. God graphed greatness into my destiny, but an ungodly roadblock detoured me from getting to my destination. My identity was undiscovered and daily disappointments defeated me – pain imprisoned my ability to embrace my pattern.

About 8 years into my pastorate, God blessed me not only with a pastor, but a father. Archbishop William Hudson, III, the presiding prelate of Pilgrim Assemblies International provided me with a positive pattern. Since then, I've seen God shift my ministry and church. Thankfully, God didn't leave me patternless. My destiny is defined and I am determined to follow my *pattern*.

Chapter 2

GENERATIONAL TRAITS

Breaking Unwanted Cycles

S eeds produce a powerful source of energy. God revealed a powerful principle concerning seeds to me at an early age. Seeds break cycles. According to Luke 8:11, the seed is the word of God. Hence, all forms of seed represent God's word.

Genealogical offspring or descendants are words frequently used throughout the Bible to trace history and provide context. Even now, every family has negative and positive traits that continue from generation to generation. The unwanted traits are what we refer to as cycles, although positive traits can create cycles too.

Upon reminiscing, most of us can name the trait our family struggles with most. Oftentimes, these traits manifest themselves at similar times of our lives. Some families produce a lineage of pastors, doctors, attorneys and other unique careers that require discipline. Other families are saturated with single mothers, generational welfare, tempers, imprisonment and other misfortunes. However, these cycles can be broken. God's word teaches us that cycles plaguing our families will be broken if we plant the seed in the soil.

In Psalms 51:5, David speaks of being conceived in sin, the power of this is two-fold. When we study and connect the dots to David's life we begin to see David was biologically a bastard child. King David endured a fatherless childhood like many people do today – his experience speaks volumes to our current society.

The traditional Jewish belief is that David's family rejected him because his mother committed adultery and birthed him out of wedlock.

The traditional Jewish belief is that David's family rejected him because his mother committed adultery. They thought he was a bastard. In fact, the word "stranger" as referenced in Psalm 69:8 has the same Hebrew root as *muzar,* meaning bastard. This further explains why David wasn't included in the original set of sons, his older brothers, brought before Samuel to be anointed as king (see I Samuel chapter 16). The Bible never mentions who his biological father is – it only references his mother's husband, Jesse. Such is he case for so many young men and women today, who have step-fathers, but no known biological dads.

One of David's not so desirable generational traits becomes evident when he plots to steal Uriah's wife, Bathsheba. David's struggles show us that the cycles created within our blood line must be broken. As a result, David says, "have mercy upon me oh God, according to thy loving kindness, according to thy multitude of tender mercies." He literarily begs forgiveness for his actions with Bathsheba.

According to Psalms 51:5, David describes his own actions as a result of having been conceived in sin. When a man sows his seed into the womb of a woman, it has the potential to stop her monthly menstrual cycle with pregnancy. It is important to note, that any seed that contradicts and conflicts with God's word is not God's seed. Once we accept the sacrificed seed of God, in the person of Jesus Christ, we are no longer under the curse of sin.

However, earthly fathers help children overcome generational stumbling blocks by facing faults themselves first. We must examine ourselves by taking a closer look at the examples we set for our offspring. We cannot empower our children if we are weakened by the sins that we refuse to face, expose and overcome. When we embrace the principles of God's word and apply his seed in our lives, cycles are broken. Every cycle is broken with a seed – and that seed is God's word alone.

Every cycle is broken with a seed – and that seed is God's word alone.

Chapter 3
THE POWER OF MY PAIN
Father of Many Nations

Fatherlessness results in weakness, but the beginning of our story need not define the end. God has something more in store for those who've experienced fatherless childhoods. Our destiny is far greater than the weakness we endure. In fact, according to Psalms 68:5, God will be a father to the fatherless – he will provide the pattern.

With more than 20 million children living without their fathers, we see the social ills daily. Fatherlessness leads to a greater risk of poverty, teen pregnancy, behavioral problems, imprisonment, drop-outs, crimes, abuse and neglect. Without a pattern to prevent these statistics, people experience the pain of fatherlessness and feel powerless.

Fatherlessness leads to a greater risk of poverty, teen pregnancy, behavioral problems, imprisonment, drop-outs, crimes, abuse and neglect.

My personal story reflects how God will produce power out of our pain. Power is defined as the ability to do something or change something. Pain is suffering or discomfort caused by injury, illness or emotional distress. Without my painful experiences, I would not have been able to accomplish my goals or fulfill my ambitions. Fatherlessness causes unwanted pain, but it also produces expected results for individuals who don't allow obstacles to stand in our way. We can either surrender to the statistics that imprison so many people in powerlessness or allow our pain to empower us. It's often said, "No pain, no gain."

I have no childhood memories of my biological father. I've been told that he saw me as a 1-year-old infant. Afterward, he saw me again as an 18-years-old. By then, I was already emotionally damaged and suffering from the pain of having no pattern. Sometimes, not having a pattern can cause a person to want to self-destruct. In fact, I attempted my first suicide as a teenager. My childhood was challenging, but I survived.

The only honorable father-figure I knew was my grandfather, *the late* Reverend Clarence Lobdell, Sr.. He maintained a great reputation, he exercised loving-kindness to all, and he served as the senior pastor of New Hope M.B. Church. In many regards, he was my hero prior to passing. Now, I walk in his footprints as the senior pastor of the same church. However, the journey of transforming my pain into power was long and difficult.

By the time I was 10-years-old, I'd experienced verbal and physical abuse, including a broken arm.

My mother married a man named Armah Roberts. As my stepfather, he adopted me as a 2-year-old and gave me his name, "Roberts". Prior to the adoption, my surname was Lobdell (after my grandfather), and then Akins, which is my biological father's last name. By the time I was 10-years-old, I'd experienced verbal and physical abuse, including a broken arm. Armah was quite cruel during that season of life. At age 11, my mother packed our bags and we left. Once again, I was fatherless. In recent years, Armah redeemed himself – I forgave him. He visited our home and church. He walked my sister down her wedding aisle, and attended my sons' sports events. We are no longer in a bad place and share positive memories. Although we've turned our pain into a powerful experience, he will never fit the description or pattern of a functional father.

The pain continued spiraling downward. During my childhood, I also had an extremely influential cousin named, Charles (Chucky) Snowden, III. He was like an older brother - we lived in the same home and shared a bedroom growing up. At the age of 22, Chucky was murdered in his home in Gary, Indiana. Seeing all of this through the eyes of a 15-old-year boy wounded me deeply. The pain that emerged in my life by the time I was 18-years-old was tremendously heartbreaking.

Patterns transcend from one generation to the next without consciousness, consent or consideration.

I didn't realize that God had a way of transforming pain into power. He has many ways of healing our brokenness and giving us greater purpose. Sometimes God uses our parents, and then sometimes he separates us from them. Abraham (Abram) was instructed by God to leave his mother, father and homeland. God promised to guide him sight unseen to an unknown place (see Genesis chapter 12). This powerful scenario reveals how God sometimes removes sons and daughters away form moms and dads to accomplish his perfect work. God is omniscient – he knows exactly what we need.

Abram's father, Terah, was a pagan worshipper, whose name meant *delay*. Its amazing how God loves us so much that he will strategically separate us from patterns that will delay our destiny. As intimidating as it must have been for Abram to leave the pattern he was familiar with, he followed God's instruction. As a result, God changed his name from Abram to Abraham, making him the father of many nations.

Patterns are powerful. Patterns transcend from one generation to the next without consciousness, consent or consideration. Consider the successions of generations from Abraham to Jacob. Abraham lied about Sarah being his wife. Isaac and Rebecca's marriage was based on lies. Jacobs name literally means deceiver or liar. Ten of Jacobs children lied about Joseph being dead. Abraham favored Ishmael, Isaac favored Esau, Jacob favored Joseph, and then Benjamin. Yet, Abraham, Isaac and Jacob were all of favored by God. Patterns do not ask for permission, nor do they seek approval. Patterns are like our fingerprints; they define our identity.

Patterns are like our fingerprints; they define our identity.

Like Abraham, God favors me. As a result, I take fatherhood seriously – and so should we all. It is my desire to establish proper patterns for my children to follow. Since I've start pastoring, God has allowed me to impact the lives of countless people who are fatherless and fractured. Once God turns our pain into power, he encourages and expects us to empower others to fulfill their destiny as well.

Just as I've been transformed from a patternless pain-filled boy to a powerful man of God, so can you. Purpose is what empowers us. Unfortunately, sometimes we go through some of life's most challenges circumstances to discover patterns of purpose.

Chapter 4

DEADBEAT DADS

The Pattern, the Beat and the Rhythm

Everybody wants a blueprint or pattern to follow in life. Without a pattern, life loses its rhythm. A rhythm is a strong, regular, repeated pattern of movement or sound. Our heartbeats create the most important rhythm we will ever experience – it signifies the strength that supports life. The term "Deadbeat Dad" is reserved for fathers that do not contribute or impart anything into their child's life.

> # Some deadbeat dads are merely repeating the cycles of previous generations. Others have been abandoned themselves.

Unfortunately, there are multiple reasons different fathers don't contribute time, talents or treasures. Some deadbeat dads are merely repeating the cycles of previous generations. Others have been abandoned themselves. While every situation is unique, a poor relationship with the mother is a common cause. Despite any excuse, there is no acceptable excuse to deprive our children from being exposes to a proper pattern.

Absentee dads interrupt the rhythm of our lives. As a result, chaos, confusion and commotion echo in the hearts of fatherless children across the country. In 2016, the average salary of a single mother was just over $35,000. This meant most single-mothers lived just over the poverty line. Raising children single-handedly, without the emotional or economic support of a spouse is a strain. Unwanted stress occurs when dads disappear – life loses its rhythm – the paternal pattern is lost. These difficulties are detrimental and the damage is irreversible. Catching up on child support will never serve as a substitute for having an active father in the life of every child. Children need their dads even more than they need their financial support.

Catching up on child support will never serve as a substitute for having an active father in the life of every child.

Whenever we identify widows in the Bible, multiple sorrows are implied. Widows experience the loss of a husband, likely the loss of their children's father, and the elimination of an entire economic system. The pattern fades when the father dies. In so much, that sons who had been shown the pattern often filled in for deceased fathers (see Luke 7:11-17).

As fathers, our existence and involvement is the blueprint for our offspring.

Absent fathers fail to embrace the responsibility of functioning within the rhythm of fatherhood. Deadbeat dads miss out on the amazing lives their children have been blessed to live. As fathers, our existence and involvement is the blueprint for our offspring. Every child, boys and girls alike, need their dads. Fatherlessness is living a life without rhythm – it is so important not to be a deadbeat dad. While there is still life in the body, it's not too late to provide a pattern. Get in the rhythm of building healthy relationships. Whether your offspring is a child or adult, your presence as a father is far more powerful than the human mind can conceive.

Chapter 5

CHILD SUPPORT

vs.

LIFE SUPPORT

The Consequences of Absent Fathers

C hild support verses life support is an important topic of discussion that must be addressed. Our current generation of fatherhood is in crisis, and our children are suffering on life support. Our children are dying, both naturally and spiritually.

Our current generation of fatherhood is in crisis, and our children are suffering on life support.

Providing support for others is a concept of bearing part of the burden or weight. Sometimes support means carrying all of the responsibilities. Support is the reality of holding up another person. Although the Bible references women as weaker vessels, it also describes their role as the ones who undergird their spouses. According to Ephesians 5:22, wives should submit themselves to their husbands. The words submit suggests to get under or support. It's interesting that the weaker vessel is asked to provide the support, but in many cases, she carries the weight of the entire family.

Our church facility is built to occupy 1,100 people. The 200 seat balcony is supported by two small beams. Without these small beams the balcony would collapse. The idea of something being the weaker vessel doesn't mean it is of any less significance. Builders and architects understand this concept well.

Building a solid and functional family is similar to erecting a construction project – it takes strategy and energy.

Building a solid and functional family is similar to erecting a construction project – it takes strategy and energy. According to the demand of seismic concept design, frame structures should have a *strong-column-weak-beam* concept. Column, in most cases, serves as decoration and support. In ancient Egypt, these columns were usually large, circular and massive structures. A beam is a structural element that primarily resists loads. So, the beam, though not as strong as the column, is equally as important to the overall structure. The one is meaningless without the other – they complete one another. Likewise, wives are as equally as relevant as their husbands. Without the strong *column* (husband) *weak-beam* (wife) concept relationships collapse. To build a healthy and happy home, men and women must both understand how their roles work together. Without this concept, families fail to possess a proper life support.

Parents should always be present to provide social, emotional, spiritual and financial support. It's unfortunate that for many children money is the least of their worries. They have no patterns. They are walking into demise, death traps and drug dens. They own guns, get imprisoned and bounce from bad relationships to worse ones. This happens everyday when children lack support and patterns. Life is not a freelance experiment – fathers provide the energy needed for life support. Fathers are unconsciously and independently designed to provide patterns for their children to follow – fathers are a key blueprint for future outcomes. However, kids need both dads and moms.

My mom, Delpha Roberts, struggled, but she survived. In fact, we all survived because of her. In the beginning, she needed food stamps to feed us month-by-month. While raising three fatherless children, she put herself through school. It wasn't easy, but she never quit. Upon receiving her Degree in

Respiratory Therapy, she earned a medical position that produced enough income to keep our heads above water, financially speaking. I didn't have everything I wanted, neither did anyone else I knew. However, I remember being embarrassed at times, because we seemed to have less than most. I recall harboring a heavy-duty sense of anger watching her work tirelessly without having help. She stayed positive and did what she had to do – and she did her best. Even still, countless times I contemplated and attempted suicide because of the lack of a father – I needed a pattern. While the lack of money and daily struggles cannot be overlooked, we can't ignore the reality of kids having identity crisis. When fathers fail to encourage the dreams and desires of their children, the outcomes are usually disastrous, deadly, and disappointing.

Even still, countless times I contemplated and attempted suicide because of the lack of father – I needed a pattern.

Single-mothers are to be commended. Mothers that support their children alone and bear the entire weight of raising kids should be applauded. Likewise, fathers who maneuver around shame and humiliation to cradle their children deserve recognition. Such fathers who step-up to the plate, providing patterns and fulfilling promises should be praised.

I should know. I continued to long for a functional relationship with my biological father. I searched for him. I found him. I prayed and I reached out. Yet, he continues to miss out. God has blessed me with a loving and beautiful wife, amazingly smart and gifted children, the most adorable grand-daughter, a thriving ministry, and so much more. I am his offspring, but he remains my absence father. I have unknown siblings. I have family that denies their own bloodline as though my existence defies their dignity. Yet, God remains my father. I cannot pretend as though my earthly father doesn't matter to me – he does very much so – he is still my pattern. Instead of shaming him, I wait patiently, with hopes that someday we will unite. I will give him chance after chance, because I understand the importance of having a pattern in your life. Meanwhile, God has adopted me as his son. *"God decided in advance to adopt us into his own family by bringing us to himself through Jesus Christ. This is what he wanted to do, and it gave him great pleasure"*

(Ephesians 1:5). I have a family of faith, a family of believers, and I am a family member in the body of Christ – and this gives me great pleasure.

"When my father and my mother forsake me, then the Lord will take me up" (Psalm 27:10).

There are so many children of God that will change this world. This transformation will transpire because God esteems life support over child support – our lives matter to God. As a result, he provides a pattern to those that are without one. *"When my father and my mother forsake me, then the Lord will take me up"* (Psalm 27:10). God has a remedy to circumvent the consequences of absent fathers.

Chapter 6

THE FATHER'S BLESSING

The Transfer from Fathers to Sons

F athers unquestionably have the ability to bless their son. This concept is quite powerful. Although this kind of blessing is often overlooked in modern society. The devastation, defeat and difficulties I faced because of my father's absence continues to impact my life. As a result, in part, this is why I possess an ambition to insure that my words, deeds and presence bless my sons. This is a long term tradition of many ancient cultures.

Fathers unquestionably have the ability to bless their son.

According to the Greek, the word blessed means to "be extremely happy". The Hebrew understanding of the word blessed means "to speak well of". (In the Foreword of this book, Pastor Keion Henderson explains this theory quite well). In addition to the pattern provided by fathers, which comes naturally, unconsciously and unintentionally, blessing our children requires effort. This should be the goal of every father – speak well of your children. The Blessing of the father is both natural and spiritual. "A good man leaves an inheritance for their children" (Proverbs 13:22). We should find peace in knowing that our fathers have taken care of our natural needs. We should also rest assured that our fathers have spoken promises into our future.

Having a father is supposed to be beneficial. Fathers should not be absent, invisible, or non-influential entities. What kind of father are you?

Having a father is supposed to be beneficial. Fathers should not be absent, invisible, or non-influential entities. What kind of father are you? Children should not wander lost without patterns. The kind of struggles and disappointments I faced as a child are inexcusable and unacceptable – all children deserve better than that. Neglect and rejection are two forms of dysfunction that my children will not intentionally experience from me. Nobody is perfect, but all committed dads must be responsible and accountable.

Responsibility and accountability has everything to do with our duty to deal with things and our obligation to explain ourselves. As fathers, we have both the abilities to provide patterns and bless our babies with a lifetime of leadership. This impartation of power to our children should spark an added sense of joy in our spirit. We have the power to supply their natural needs and provide spiritual blessings to our sons and daughters.

As fathers, we have both the abilities to provide patterns and bless our babies with a lifetime of leadership.

Isaac wanted to ensure that he blessed his oldest son Esau, but was tricked into blessing Jacob. Afterward, Jacob did something similar as his father. He crossed his hands and blessed the younger of the next generation, which was against custom – but he followed the pattern. Blessings, gifts, customs, traits and anointing are all generational blueprints passed on from fathers. Patterns are always transferable, sometimes the impartation happens intentionally, and others times the results exceed our understanding.

Patterns are always transferable, sometimes the impartation happens intentionally, and others times the results exceed our understanding.

For example, despite the fact that I have no relationship with my father, I'm aware of his lifestyle as a preacher – clearly there is a pattern. My grandfather, Clarence Lobdell, Sr., died, yet I inherited my preaching ability, my pastorate and my parenting skills strictly from his influence. Afterward, Archbishop William Hudson, III started imparting into my life as a father in 2012. His presence and involvement is refreshing and fulfilling. His spiritual impartations transfer with ease. My personal ministry began to evolve and change for the better. My personal growth was unequivocally the result of his influence. Archbishop Hudson passed a mantle to me, laid hands on me, and spoke life into my wounded and dying soul. God used him to provide for me in a way that only a father could. Undoubtedly, God was speaking well of me and it made me extremely happy.

Chapter 7

GOD IS MY FATHER

The Pattern of Prayer

God does all things well. There is no failure in him. It is written in Psalms 139:14, "we were fearfully and wonderfully made." It is important to understand that when God made man, he gave us our own will. Therefore, despite God's perfect design, we still have the ability to deviate from his ideal plan. There is a contrast between the

God does all things well. There is no failure in him. The scripture says in Psalms 139:14, we were fearfully and wonderfully made.

awesomeness he put in us and the frailty of flesh. That being said, herein is the reason for this book. All fathers have patterns to pass on to their children. Unfortunately, some men make the decision not to do so. Such is not God's will, although many men make poor choices. We must learn to be God-like and do a better job providing perfect patterns to our children.

The apostle Paul writes in II Corinthians 4:7, "We have this treasure in earthen vessels, that the excellency of the power may be of God not us." God puts treasure in flawed flesh – and this was no mistake. However, we make mistakes. Even involved fathers with tremendous treasures sometimes fail to demonstrate and display examples of the proper patterns.

Even involved fathers with tremendous treasures sometimes fail to demonstrate and display examples of the proper patterns.

Here's why. There answer is simple. We are not God. Ultimately, God has the master pattern and does not make mistakes. The choices we make have the ability to restrain, restrict and regulate the destiny of our children. As a result, I needed deliverance. Part of my deliverance included not feeling sorry for myself. I had to realize that even in the absence of my biological father, despite the abuse of my stepfather, God did not leave me fatherless. He has always been my father.

According to Proverbs 3:5-6, we must trust in the lord with our whole heart and lean not to our own understanding. God want us to acknowledge him, and then he will direct our path. God makes it clear that when we seek him he will not leave us patternless. God has a perfect plan and a promising purpose for our lives.

Unquestionably, God is our Father – he designed the blueprint for our lives, he has the plans for our future and he dictates the pattern we will follow. In the gospel of Mathew chapter 6, the disciples asked the Lord to teach them how to communicate with the Creator.

Afterward, Christ showed them the pattern of prayer. We must always start by acknowledging God's identity as our father. The reason I've been able to triumph over the neglect, abuse, suicidal thoughts, divorce, unforgiveness and plethora of personal mistakes is because I acknowledge our heavenly father first.

This book is written to strengthen suffering sons, daughters, moms and dads alike. Even if your life is absent of manmade patterns, be encouraged to emerge out of the dust of absent dads. Despite any difficulty, don't quit. You are not inadequate. You are not a mistake. You are wonderfully made. There is a perfect plan, purpose and pattern for your life. Always acknowledge our heavenly father as the navigator, and you will walk into your destiny. God is our father and he does all things well.

We must always start by acknowledging God's identity as our father.

Chapter 8

I AM ESTABLISHED

Amongst Two or Three Witnesses

O ne of the many scriptures that consistently possess a personal and profound affect on my life is I Peter 5:10. This scripture reveals one of the four-fold promises of God regarding suffering. After we've suffered, God promises to *establish* us. The Greek word used to describe the word establish means to confirm, fix, set like concrete, strengthen and make firm. Notice how this is the result of, and only takes place after suffering occurs.

The Greek word used to describe the word *establish* means to confirm, fix, set like concrete, strengthen and make firm.

Without question, statistics illustrate how the lack of patterns or active fathers cause suffering. Fatherlessness uncovers children and exposes them to negativities, uncertainties and perverted pleasantries. Some sufferings have been assigned to our blueprint even when fathers are present. In fact, some children suffer at the hands of their fathers.

With no uncertainty, these sufferings are not senseless, they are spiritually prescribed to produce a permanent and positive result. God is using our unwanted circumstances, difficult challenges and hurtful crisis as criteria to qualify us for indescribable blessings. God will establish us, so don't get bitter, knowing that God is going to make us better.

How amazing is that? Our suffering is not in vain. After feeling the kind of emptiness and loneliness that caused heartache, headache and hurt, God intervened. Prior to God's intervention, the emotional turmoil was so great that I want my life to end. Instead, he used my pain to engraft me as a permanent fixture as a leader amongst many. God set me up. He confirmed me. Affirmation is key because countless children are looking for self-identity and confirmation. Oftentimes, we need to hear others endorse, identify, and make mention of our existence.

Affirmation is key because countless children are looking for self-identity and confirmation.

In the mouth of two or three witnesses let every word be established (see II Corinthians 13:1). Daughters fall for the wrong men and suffer unhealthy relationships trying to find their identity. Sons make careless mistakes because absent fathers leave no blueprint for life. Children need a pattern – fathers provide that pattern. We need to hear the voice of our earthly fathers echoing the sentiments of our heavenly father over our lives.

Children need a pattern – fathers provide that pattern.

There is a Roman law that says, one witness is as good as no witnesses. The word testimony in the Latin root means witness. It comes from the word testis, as in witness. Whether by deed, duty or denial, our fathers will result in the reason why we are established. Our physical anatomy also confirms this reality. Men are designed with two testicles, and our children are established based on our witness concerning God's plan for their lives.

When we come into this world, there is no vote taken for what we will become. Once we accept Christ, we must be willing to endure suffering in order to evolve into the creation he intended. Be encouraged, the best is yet to come. An upcoming generation of fathers will gain a deeper understanding of fatherhood and redefine what godly families look like. Patterns are powerful. God will never leave you without a blueprint. This book contains the recipe to prepare individuals to succeed. Whether you are the father or the child, all human life revolves around the concept of patterns. When we suffer, our blueprints, plans, purpose and patterns are established.

ABOUT THE AUTHOR
BISHOP SIEON C. ROBERTS, SR.

* * *

Bishop Sieon Roberts is the overseer of New Hope Church in Gary, Indiana. He is the proud husband of Anita Roberts, as well as an actively involved father. This book, Where is My Father, is the newest of a four book collection by the author. He also published Panting After His Presence, Teen Rocks, and Discipleship. Bishop Roberts aspires to use literature to educate, encourage and empower. For speaking engagements, contact Bishop Sieon C. Roberts, Sr. at 219-883-5743 or e-mail reginanewhope@gmail.com.

* * *

WHERE IS MY FATHER
The Missing Pattern

Made in the USA
Middletown, DE
29 June 2019